Original title:
Winter? More Like "Brr-ter"

Copyright © 2024 Creative Arts Management OÜ
All rights reserved.

Author: Julian Carmichael
ISBN HARDBACK: 978-9916-94-288-8
ISBN PAPERBACK: 978-9916-94-289-5

Gliding on a Frozen Lake

Silent glide on ice so clear,
Whispers of winter fill the air.
Footprints trace a fleeting dance,
In this stillness, all entranced.

Moonlight glimmers on the sheen,
Nature's canvas, crisp and clean.
Breath like fog, both soft and light,
In this moment, pure delight.

Embracing the Chill of Twilight

Twilight blankets all around,
Shadows stretch upon the ground.
Colors fade to deepening blue,
Stars awaken, bright and true.

Cold winds whisper through the trees,
Carrying tales on the freeze.
Embrace the chill, let it flow,
As night wraps all in its glow.

Slumbering Under the Glittering Gaze

Snowflakes drift from skies above,
Blanketing the world we love.
Gentle dreams in winter's keep,
The earth lies down in quiet sleep.

Stars peek through the frosty veil,
Their sparkling whispers tell a tale.
Nature waits, beneath the snow,
In slumber's peace, all life will grow.

Haiku of a Winter Night

Winter moonlit sky,
Branches creak with quiet grace,
Whispers in the snow.

The Deepening Chill of December

The air grows thin, a whispering night,
Stars shimmer dim, in fading light.
Frost clings tight to the window pane,
Nature waits, for snow, for rain.

Trees stand bare, their branches stark,
Silence wraps around the park.
Footsteps crunch on powdered ground,
In December's grip, peace is found.

Snowflakes and Sighs

Snowflakes dance, a gentle fall,
Each one unique, they heed the call.
Laughter echoes, beneath the gray,
Children play, in winter's sway.

With every breath, a cloud of white,
Sighs escape into the night.
Warmth resides in hearts so bright,
As snow drapes softly, pure delight.

The Solstice of Stillness

Shadows lengthen, the day grows shy,
Time slows down, as moments fly.
Winter's solstice, a pause so grand,
Nature holds a quiet hand.

A stillness deep, the world at rest,
In solemn peace, we feel so blessed.
The longest night, a sacred time,
Reflecting life, in silent rhyme.

Fire's Dance Against the Cold

Crackling flames, a flickering glow,
Casting warmth in the evening's flow.
Embers leap, a dance of light,
Drawing us near on this chilly night.

Stories shared by the hearth's embrace,
Flickers of joy, in every face.
Outside the winds whisper and howl,
Inside we cherish, we laugh, we prowl.

The Cold Touch of Solitude

In the stillness of the night,
Whispers echo, faint delight.
A lone shadow walks the lane,
Wrapped in silence, fraught with pain.

Stars above, cold and bright,
Glimmers of a forgotten light.
Yet beneath the frosty air,
Yearns a heart, so unaware.

Footsteps leave a ghostly trace,
In this empty, quiet space.
Each breath a cloud, fleeting sighs,
In the echoes where hope lies.

Solitude, a bittersweet art,
Etches memories in the heart.
In the cold touch, time stands still,
A lingering ache, yet a will.

Icicle Dreams and Frosted Schemes

Glistening like jewels on high,
Icicles dance, the winter's cry.
Each crystal a story, a theme,
Whispers of sweet, silent dreams.

Frosted schemes in the pale dawn,
Sunlight kisses the sparkles drawn.
Nature weaves her lace with grace,
In this enchanted, frozen space.

Beneath the weight of the snow,
Secrets of the night bestow.
Shadows play in the chilly breeze,
Dancing softly among the trees.

In the heart of the gleaming cold,
Stories of adventure unfold.
Icicle dreams, forever gleam,
Life embedded in winter's scheme.

Winter's Gentle Nudge

A tender whisper on the ground,
Winter nudges, softly sounds.
Each flake falls like a gentle kiss,
Moments wrapped in frosty bliss.

Branches bow with a silver coat,
Nature sighs, as snowflakes float.
Quietly falling, time stands still,
Winter brings her graceful will.

Children laugh, their voices play,
Snowball fights in bright array.
Joy ignites as the world transforms,
A wonderland in winter's arms.

Underneath the starry sky,
Dreams take flight, they soar and fly.
Winter's nudge, a sweet embrace,
Awakens hope in every space.

Blankets of Silence and Snow

Blankets draped on earth so wide,
Snowflakes settle, softly glide.
Nature wraps her arms around,
In hushed whispers, peace is found.

Footpaths hidden, secrets kept,
In the silence, memories crept.
Crystals glimmer under the moon,
A silver song, a midnight tune.

Trees adorned in white array,
Hold the warmth of yesterday.
Beneath the frost, life waits in hush,
While the world slows down in a gentle rush.

In this realm of soft and white,
Hearts warm up, igniting light.
Blankets of silence, pure and deep,
Cradle dreams, as the world sleeps.

A Dance of Frost and Fire

In twilight's breath, the embers glow,
Frost whispers secrets, soft and slow.
Dancing shadows twist and sway,
Lost in dreams where night meets day.

Crimson flames ignite the night,
While icy patterns shine so bright.
A waltz of fire, a shimmer of ice,
Nature's beauty, a sweet paradise.

Stars above, like diamonds, twirl,
Fires crackle, icy winds swirl.
In the heart, warmth finds a way,
Frost and fire in grand ballet.

Night unveils its mystic grace,
In the dance, no time, no space.
Frost and flame in harmony,
Whispers of love, eternally.

The Sorrow of Bare Branches

In winter's clutch, the branches bare,
Whispering loss in the chilling air.
Each twig a memory, sharp and stark,
Echoing silence, a tender mark.

Frosted crowns where leaves once thrived,
In solitude, the heart has strived.
Yet beneath the cold, hope will find,
New roots forming, a love entwined.

Raindrops kiss the earth with tears,
A soft lament for fading years.
Through barren limbs, the sun will shine,
Renewing life, a sacred sign.

As seasons shift, the branches sway,
A promise etched in every ray.
Though sorrow lingers, joy will bloom,
In the embrace that lifts the gloom.

Journey Through a Crystal Labyrinth

Amidst the gleam of ice and glass,
Footsteps echo as moments pass.
A maze of frost that sparkles bright,
Beneath the glow of pale moonlight.

Each corner turned reveals a dream,
Shattered light in a silent stream.
Winding paths of sharp delight,
Leading wanderers through the night.

In the heart of this frosty maze,
Memories flicker, lost in haze.
Hope glimmers like stars above,
Guiding souls to find their love.

With every turn, a story told,
In crystal dreams, the brave are bold.
Through the labyrinth, a heart will roam,
Finding solace, finally home.

Dim Light on Snowy Pathways

In twilight's embrace, the pathways gleam,
Beneath the hush, a soft moonbeam.
Footprints whisper on snowy trails,
Tales of winter, as the silence exhales.

Frost-kissed edges, each step aligns,
In the canvas white where wonder shines.
Shadows stretch with a gentle sway,
Blending night into breaking day.

Lanterns flicker in the crisp night air,
Casting warmth in the chill, so rare.
Through the dim, a heartbeat calls,
Drawing seekers within its thrall.

Wander through the drifts of light,
Seeking solace in the night.
On snowy pathways, dreams ignite,
In the embrace of soft twilight.

The World in a Crystal Veil

A glimmering hush, the dawn unfolds,
Each breath is a shimmer, the night it holds.
Whispers of frost on branches sway,
Wrapped in a blanket of silver and gray.

Each moment caught in a glistening thread,
Nature's soft canvas, untouched, widespread.
A world of whispers, secrets untold,
Framed in a crystal, a sight to behold.

The sun peeks gently, a warm embrace,
Glistening diamonds, a shimmering lace.
Time seems to linger, a delicate sigh,
In the quiet magic, where moments fly.

Awake in the stillness, dreams come alive,
In this radiant vessel, we quietly thrive.
With each step taken, a journey begins,
In the crystal veil, where beauty spins.

Embracing the Icy Quiet

A shroud of stillness, the world asleep,
Wrapped in a blanket that promises keep.
Snowflakes dance softly, touching the ground,
In the icy quiet, peace can be found.

Branches all bowed, under winter's weight,
Silence surrounds, a serene escape.
Every sound muffled, a gentle embrace,
In the icy quiet, worries erase.

Footsteps are whispers on powdery white,
Each stride a heartbeat, so pure, so light.
Moments stretch onward, like shadows that creep,
In the realm of silence, secrets we keep.

Time slows down here, in the frosty air,
Embracing the stillness, free from all care.
With eyes wide open, we gaze at the scene,
Finding solace in spaces serene.

Laughter in the Snow

Children all gather, joy in the air,
Snowmen are building, laughter they share.
Sleds flying down hills with gleeful shouts,
A chorus of giggles, echoing about.

Snowflakes are falling, a dance in the light,
Each one a treasure, pure and so bright.
Warm mittens waving, bright scarves that blow,
In the heart of winter, let happiness flow.

Huddled together, a snowball fight,
Joyful exclamations, a beautiful sight.
The chill in the air, it sparkles with glee,
In the laughter of children, the spirit runs free.

Evening descends, the day starts to wane,
Footprints in snow, like whispers remain.
Memories linger as stars start to glow,
In the laughter of winter, our spirits will grow.

Frost-etched Reflections

Windows adorned with delicate lace,
Frost-etched patterns that time can't erase.
Nature's artwork, a moment of grace,
Whispers of winter that softly embrace.

Each breath is a cloud, a fleeting dream,
Capturing stillness in sunlight's gleam.
The world outside, a beautiful chill,
Frost-etched reflections, a quiet thrill.

In the calm of the morning, a gentle display,
The beauty of nature in twilight's ballet.
Glimmers of frost on each surface lie,
Mirrors of magic beneath the sky.

As day turns to night, peace takes its place,
In the heart of winter, a warm warm space.
Frost-etched reflections, a moment to pause,
Nature's own art, deserving applause.

When Silence Falls in Sparkling Flakes

When silence falls like gentle snow,
Whispers dance in the soft, cool glow.
Each flake a story, quiet and bright,
Embracing the world in purest white.

The night unfolds with a shimmering hush,
As the stars above begin their lush.
Under their gaze, the stillness breathes,
While dreams awaken in tangled wreaths.

Footsteps are muted, echoing low,
Carried away on the winter's flow.
In this serenity, time seems to freeze,
Wrapped in the magic of winter's tease.

With each falling flake, the heart finds peace,
As silence cradles and sorrows cease.
In this enchanted, frosty ballet,
We find our hopes in the cold's soft sway.

The Echoes of Shushed Streets

In the heart of night, where shadows creep,
The streetlamps glow, secrets to keep.
Echoes whisper through empty lanes,
In the stillness, the city regains.

Footsteps linger, a fleeting sound,
As the moonlight blankets the ground.
Each corner holds a quiet tale,
When silence prevails, dreams set sail.

Beneath the stars, a tranquil sigh,
To the rhythm of night, we softly fly.
Where echoes linger and memories play,
Guiding our hearts in a timeless sway.

A ballet of shadows and soft, sweet beams,
Unfolding stories spun from dreams.
As the world silently breaths a tune,
Our hearts align with the rhythm of June.

Beneath a Blanket of Pearl

Beneath a blanket of shimmering pearl,
The world transforms in a soft, white swirl.
Every edge softened, each sound wrapped tight,
In the magic that comes with the cloak of night.

The landscape glistens, a silken sheet,
Every step taken is light and sweet.
A hush descends where hoarfrost gleams,
Wrapping the world in delicate dreams.

Trees bow low with a weight of grace,
Nature's beauty, a tranquil embrace.
In this serene, snowy delight,
Hearts find warmth in the cool twilight.

As snowflakes drift, each one unique,
They carry stories that softly speak.
Under a canopy, pure and unbroken,
Whispers of winter, softly spoken.

Fables Told by the Frost

Fables told by the frost at dawn,
Patterns painted on the lawn.
Each icy breath a tale to share,
Crafting wonders everywhere.

In the crisp air, the stories spin,
Of nights long gone and where we've been.
A tapestry woven in chilly thread,
Through whispered legends, salt and lead.

Frozen branches arch with pride,
Silent watchers, as dreams collide.
In the heart of winter, we learn to see,
Fables whispering of what could be.

With each droplet that drips away,
Life unfolds in hidden play.
In the frost's embrace, our memories blend,
As time weaves tales that never end.

Chill of the Frosted Dawn

The sun peeks through a silver haze,
While frost lays claim to long, cold days.
Whispers of winter fill the air,
A quiet magic resting everywhere.

Barren branches glisten bright,
Crystals reflecting morning's light.
Each breath clouds in the early glow,
The chill of dawn begins to show.

Icicles Whisper Secrets

From rooftops hang the shimmering ice,
They catch the sun, a frozen slice.
With every drip, a tale they weave,
Nature's art, hard to believe.

Listen close to their gentle song,
Whispers of winter, soft and strong.
Each sparkling drop writes a line,
In the frigid air, they softly shine.

Snowflakes on Silent Streets

Falling gently, a soft embrace,
Snowflakes dance, a timeless grace.
Blankets white on streets once bare,
A hush of magic fills the air.

Footsteps muffled in the night,
A world transformed, pure and bright.
In every flake, a story told,
In the quiet, memories unfold.

Frosty Mornings

The world awakens, frost-kissed and clear,
Morning's chill brings the winter near.
Coffee brews with a warming cheer,
As icy breath engulfs the year.

Windows frosted, patterns unique,
Nature's craft, a chance to sneak.
Into the heart of a brisk delight,
Frosty mornings, pure and bright.

Cozy Hearts

In the glow of a crackling fire,
Hearts unite, spirits aspire.
Wrapped in blankets, warm and snug,
Love ignites with every hug.

Outside, the snow falls soft and light,
Inside, the warmth ignites the night.
Cozy moments, shared and sweet,
In winter's arms, our hearts meet.

Quietude in a Snowbound Silence

Snowflakes whisper as they fall,
Blanketing the world in white,
A tranquil hush, a gentle call,
Where time seems to pause in light.

Trees stand tall in frosted grace,
Each branch adorned with crystal lace,
Footprints lost in soft embrace,
Nature sleeps in this quiet space.

The world utters not a sound,
Only beauty all around,
In this peace, our hearts confound,
Finding joy where love is found.

As night descends, stars twinkle bright,
Casting dreams on snowy sight,
In this calm, we hold on tight,
To moments wrapped in pure delight.

The Drawn Breath of the Frigid Air

Inhale deeply, feel the chill,
Each breath a cloud, a fleeting thrill,
The world is still, beneath the sun,
Where icy winds and warmth have spun.

Frosted fields gleam in the light,
A canvas painted, pure and white,
Each stepping forth leaves a trace,
In the crisp air, we find our place.

Birds take flight on feathered wings,
In the silence, a songbird sings,
The heart beats slow, the mind at ease,
In this moment, we find peace.

Hold on tight, for winter's song,
In its embrace, we all belong,
The drawn breath of the frigid air,
Awakens dreams beyond compare.

Icebound Reverie

Frozen ponds reflect the sky,
A mirror held where whispers lie,
In twilight's grip, the world holds still,
Dreams wander free through winter's chill.

Crystals dance on branches bare,
Whispers twirling in the air,
With every breath, memories flow,
Where hearts in silence come to know.

Shadows stretch as daylight fades,
In icy realms where beauty pervades,
Softly drifting, thoughts unite,
In an icebound reverie, pure and bright.

Twinkling stars descend like dreams,
In the stillness, nothing seems,
But a magic woven tight,
In the heart of a winter night.

Glaciers of the Heart

Beneath the ice, a story glows,
Traveling deep where no one goes,
Layers formed in time's embrace,
Glaciers of the heart find grace.

Cold as depths of winter's night,
Yet within, a warm light's bright,
The journey long, yet sweetly true,
In frozen worlds, love breaks through.

Mountains rise, and rivers freeze,
Each heartbeat like a gentle breeze,
In the silent space, we seek,
The warmth found in the still and meek.

As thawing springs begin to call,
The glaciers yield, and shadows fall,
Love's true essence, never far,
Shining bright, our guiding star.

In the Grip of the Ice Queen

With every breath, the chill descends,
Her fingers trace the frozen lands.
In silence deep, the shadows creep,
The ice queen's reign, it never ends.

A crown of frost upon her brow,
She dances through the glistening trees.
Her laughter echoes in the night,
Carried by the biting breeze.

Snowflakes swirl like whispered dreams,
Entwined in winter's soft embrace.
She weaves her spells with icy grace,
Captivating all who dare to freeze.

Yet in her heart, a secret glows,
A warmth that she has learned to hide.
For beneath the layers of her frost,
There lies a flame, her soul's true guide.

When Days Merge into Frosty Nights

The sun dips low, a muted glow,
As twilight drapes the world in white.
Beneath the stars, the chill air flows,
And whispers summon frostbitten sighs.

Hours blend where shadows roam,
In twilight's edge, time holds its breath.
Each moment casts a fleeting home,
Embracing both life and death.

From dusk till dawn, the silence hums,
The world enfolded in a dream.
Footprints claimed by winter's drums,
Echoing a soft, unyielding theme.

Yet in this cold, a spark will rise,
Igniting hearts with fierce delight.
When days all merge in frosty skies,
Hope awakens, chasing night.

The Whispered Secrets of the Cold

In the hush of winter's breath,
Soft secrets ride the biting air.
Each flake a tale of life and death,
Wrapped within a frosty snare.

Beneath the trees, the shadows play,
Whispers of ages, lost in time.
The cold reveals what hearts betray,
A soundless song, a silent rhyme.

Echoes dance on icy streams,
Stories held in frozen veins.
Nature speaks in subtle dreams,
Where warmth and chill share secret chains.

With every gust, the past returns,
Awakens paths, long left behind.
In whispered secrets, the heart learns,
What lies beneath the frost's swift bind.

Ethereal Echoes of the Frozen Forest

Whispers dance on the icy breeze,
Branches shimmer with frosty please,
Moonlight glows on the crystal floor,
Nature sings in an ancient score.

Footsteps lost in a world so white,
Trees stand tall, bathed in soft light,
Echoes linger, a haunting spell,
In this silence, stories dwell.

Snowflakes twirl like lost dreams soar,
Among the shadows that evermore,
Faintest calls from the depths of night,
Guide the wanderer with pure delight.

In the heart of the frozen woods,
Magic pulses, igniting moods,
With every breath, the air turns sweet,
Ethereal echoes, where spirits meet.

The Spectrum of Glistening Blue

Vast horizons stretch in azure hue,
Where the ocean meets the clear sky too,
Waves like whispers crest and roll,
In the depths, the heart finds soul.

From cerulean peaks to violets deep,
A tapestry of colors that never sleep,
Shadows dance in the shimmering light,
Each tone tells stories of day and night.

Silken tides caress the shore,
Every ripple, a promise of more,
In the interplay of sun and sea,
Awakening dreams, wild and free.

Beneath the depths, secrets hide,
In a world where wonders abide,
Spectrum flows with a gentle sigh,
Glistening blue, beneath the sky.

A Frigid Flare in a World of Warmth

In a realm where warmth softly glows,
A frigid flare seems to oppose,
Whispers of winter in bright sunlight,
Shattering silence, a brilliant sight.

Ice-spun flames dance in the air,
Frost-kissed wonders, a sight so rare,
With every spark, a chill ignites,
In moments where day surrenders nights.

Hearts may long for the summer's kiss,
Yet find joy in this frosty bliss,
For warmth and cold can intertwine,
Creating beauty, pure and divine.

So let the frigid spark your fire,
In the core of the heart, let it inspire,
For in every contrast, life blooms bright,
A frigid flare, a beacon of light.

Frosty Veils and Smoky Tales

Misty mornings clad in white,
Veils of frost, a sheer delight,
Stories linger in the chilled air,
Whispers hidden, everywhere.

Pine trees wrapped in gauzy frost,
Echoes of warmth, though winter's tossed,
Wisps of smoke curl through the trees,
Carrying whispers of winter's freeze.

Each tale woven in frost and fog,
Resonates like a fleeting dog,
Chasing dreams through the icy veil,
Magic brews in every wail.

So let the frosty tales unfold,
A world hidden in stories told,
In each breath, let the magic sail,
Through frosty veils and smoky tales.

Chills in the Evening Air

The twilight whispers softly now,
As shadows dance, the cold winds bow.
A shiver runs through every street,
With every breath, the night feels sweet.

The moon hangs low, a silver disk,
Wrapped in a fog, so soft, so brisk.
Each gust of wind, a gentle sigh,
The stars appear in the velvet sky.

Footsteps crunch on frozen ground,
Where calm and quiet can be found.
A world transformed in dusky hues,
As night takes hold, we breathe the blues.

The evening air, a sacred song,
Where moments pause, and time feels long.
In every chill, there's warmth to share,
In whispers held in evening air.

Serene Silence of Sleet

The world is wrapped in silver threads,
As winter's grip so lightly spreads.
Each flake a whisper, soft and sweet,
In serene silence, all is neat.

Beneath the trees, a gentle hush,
While nature holds its quiet blush.
In stillness lies a perfect peace,
As sleet falls down, our cares release.

The echo of the softest fall,
A tranquil call, a soothing thrall.
In winter's grasp, we tend to stay,
As dreamers drift till break of day.

In every flake, a story spun,
Where time pauses, and warmth is won.
The serene silence paints the night,
A canvas blank, a pure delight.

A Symphony of Cold and Calm

In muted tones, the ice does sing,
A melody of winter's ring.
The frost weaves through each branch and bough,
Creating silence, soft and low.

Each note a chill that lingers sweet,
As evening draws its cool retreat.
A symphony, both sharp and clear,
In winter's grasp, all hearts draw near.

The quiet hum of frozen air,
Enfolds us in its tender care.
Where whispers float like feathered dreams,
And time stands still, or so it seems.

As stars converge in velvet space,
We find our solace, a warm embrace.
In this concert, hearts align,
A symphony where most feel fine.

Frost-kissed Memories

The morning breaks with frosty breath,
Where whispers blend with scents of death.
Old memories dance in crispy air,
A fleeting glimpse, both bright and rare.

Each moment trapped in icy hold,
The past returns, both brave and bold.
Through silver mist and sparkling light,
We cherish warmth in winter's bite.

In laughter shared, our spirits soar,
Through frosted fields, we learn and explore.
Every touch, a memory we keep,
In frost-kissed echoes, dreams run deep.

As nature weaves her tapestry,
We find ourselves in history.
Each frost-kissed flake, a tale retold,
In this embrace, our hearts feel bold.

The Frigid Kiss of Nightfall

The day retreats, a whispered sigh,
As shadows stretch beneath the sky.
A chill descends, the stars ignite,
A frigid kiss, the veil of night.

Frosted breath upon the air,
Dreams awaken, stripped and bare.
In silence deep, the world will pause,
A moment held, without a cause.

The moonlight casts a silver trace,
Each shadow dances with its grace.
In twilight's arms, old secrets weave,
A story shared, yet hard to believe.

In the still, the heart does race,
A world transformed in night's embrace.
We linger here, where time stands still,
In the frigid kiss, we find our will.

Chilling Memories in a Snowdrift

In snowdrifts deep, the memories lie,
Whispers of laughter, soft and shy.
Frozen moments, captured bright,
Chilling echoes of pure delight.

Footsteps trace a path of old,
Stories whispered, yet untold.
The frostbite stings, but hearts stay warm,
In winter's grip, we find our charm.

Each flake that falls, a song of grace,
Covers the world in a silken embrace.
In chilly winds, the past unwinds,
A treasure trove of tender finds.

Wrapped in layers of snow and ice,
We chase the memory, pay the price.
In bitter cold, our spirits live,
Chilling memories, still they give.

Frosty Fractals of Time

In frosty fractals, time will bend,
Moments scattered, around the bend.
Each crystal shines, a story told,
A shimmering truth that won't grow old.

The past reflects in each sharp edge,
Within the silence, we make our pledge.
To capture joy, to hold it tight,
In frozen realms of endless night.

Ticking clocks beneath the veil,
Every heartbeat, a soft trail.
In winter's breath, we find our way,
Through frosty fractals, night and day.

Each step we take, the dance aligns,
Within the matrix of tangled lines.
A fleeting glance of what may be,
Frosty fractals, set us free.

The Stillness that Speaks

In the stillness, the echoes play,
Soft whispers of the light of day.
In hushed tones, the world reveals,
The quiet magic that it feels.

Beneath the surface, thoughts arise,
A balm of peace in starlit skies.
With every breath, we reach and grasp,
The stillness wraps us in its clasp.

The trees remain in silent sway,
As time unfolds in its gentle way.
A moment paused, as shadows tease,
In stillness found, we find our ease.

Let silence speak, and hearts will listen,
In everyday grace, our souls glisten.
In stillness, truth begins to gleam,
A hidden wisdom, soft as a dream.

The Quiet Majesty of Hoarfrost

Delicate lace on every branch,
Winter's art, a silent trance.
Morning light is caught so bright,
Whispers of the frost's moonlight.

A world transformed, so calm, so pure,
Nature drapes a silver cure.
Footsteps soft on frozen ground,
Where beauty in stillness is found.

Breathless awe in the crisp, cool air,
Each sparkling flake, a fleeting prayer.
The quiet speaks, a timeless lore,
In hoarfrost's grip, we learn to soar.

A fleeting moment, soon to fade,
Yet in the heart, the magic stayed.
A canvas blank, white and vast,
In this serenity, shadows cast.

Sleet's Serenade on Windows

A symphony of ice and rain,
Tapping gently, a soft refrain.
Windows fog with whispered sighs,
Nature's voice in muted cries.

Each droplet dances, swift and swift,
Painting tales in a frosty script.
Sleet cascades like silver streams,
A lullaby for restless dreams.

Chords of winter, a tender song,
In this melody, we belong.
The world outside is cloaked and grey,
Yet in our hearts, warmth will stay.

Embrace the chill, let silence fall,
In the symphony, we hear the call.
A serenade of time and space,
In sleet's soft touch, we find our place.

Shivers in the Starlit Sky

Whispers of night in a velvet dome,
Stars twinkle softly, far from home.
A chill that dances on the breeze,
Dreams take flight, over land and seas.

Each shimmer tells of ancient tales,
Of lovers lost and midnight trails.
The moon, a guardian, watches close,
In her glow, the universe flows.

A tapestry of light unfolds,
In the dark, a thousand stories told.
We shiver beneath this endless sight,
Finding warmth in the celestial light.

Hearts connect in the stillness fair,
Shared moments breathe in the cold night air.
As starlight drapes the earth below,
In its embrace, we gently glow.

Hearthside Reflections

Crackling embers, warmth surrounds,
In the stillness, comfort found.
Flickering flames dance and play,
A peaceful end to the busy day.

Stories shared in glowing light,
Laughter echoes, spirits bright.
Mugs of cider, sweet and warm,
Outside the chill, inside the charm.

Memories made in every spark,
Heartfelt whispers fill the dark.
In the hearth's embrace, we reside,
With tender souls, side by side.

As the fire slowly fades away,
Our bonds grow strong, come what may.
In reflections of flick'ring flame,
We find our joy, we find our name.

A Glimpse of the Frozen Moon

In the night sky, silver gleams,
A frozen moon, eternal dreams.
Casting shadows, calm and light,
Whispers softly, bold and bright.

Silent wonders fill the air,
Nature pauses, devoid of care.
Stars around, like diamonds fall,
In this moment, magic calls.

Winds do dance with icy grace,
Kissing cheeks, a tender trace.
Beneath the glow, the world stands still,
Cradled softly, heart to thrill.

A glimpse of peace, the night unveils,
In winter's breath, enchantment sails.
Moonbeams weave a silken thread,
In slumber's arms, we drift to bed.

When the World Turns White

Snowflakes falling, soft and light,
Blanketing earth in purest white.
A hush descends, serene and deep,
As the world wraps in winter's sleep.

Branches bow with heavy loads,
A quiet path where silence flows.
Footprints trace the frosty ground,
In this stillness, peace is found.

Children laugh with glee and cheer,
Creating joy as winter's near.
Snowmen rise with coal-black eyes,
Smiling under slate-gray skies.

When the world turns, magic's born,
From the dusk to early morn.
A canvas bright, all spirits lift,
In winter's heart, a precious gift.

Frosted Breath of Stillness

Teeth of ice on window pane,
Frosty breath, a whispered strain.
Nights are wrapped in silver veils,
While nature sleeps, the magic trails.

Shadows lengthen, daylight fades,
In the quiet, warmth cascades.
Softly falling, flakes descend,
Each a story, a silent friend.

Footfalls muffled, secrets kept,
While the world in wonder swept.
Candles flicker, light so sweet,
In this moment, hearts do meet.

Frosted breath, a chill so kind,
In the stillness, peace we find.
Wrapped in layers, cozy tight,
In winter's hold, we find our light.

Hibernation's Embrace

Nature's pause in slumber's clutch,
Wrapped in whispers, soft as such.
Beneath the snow, life waits and brews,
In hibernation, dreams diffuse.

Quiet moments, a tender sigh,
Under stars, the world does lie.
Bears do nest, as cold winds sigh,
While the moon remembers high.

Branches creak in icy grace,
Time moves slow in winter's pace.
Stillness deep, a sacred trust,
In this space, hope turns to dust.

Hibernation's sweet embrace,
Teaches patience, gentle grace.
In the heart of winter's call,
Life awakes with spring's installed.

Shadows of Pines Wrapped in White

Beneath the branches, silence reigns,
A blanket soft, the world contains.
Whispers of winds, in hushed refrain,
Dance through the boughs, like gentle chains.

Frost-kissed needles, glimmer bright,
Casting shadows, playing with light.
Nature's canvas, pure and slight,
Wrapped in white, a winter's sight.

Footsteps linger, in the snow,
A fleeting path where none will go.
The pines stand tall, their wisdom flow,
Guardians of dreams from long ago.

In twilight's glow, the hush prevails,
As night descends, the magic tails.
Wrapped in white, the forest trails,
With shadows of pines, the heart exhales.

The First Flurry of Fate

The first flurry catches the eye,
Softly drifting from the sky.
In each flake, a tale unfolds,
Whispers of warmth in winter's hold.

Crisp air sparkles, hope takes flight,
The world awakens in pure white.
A canvas fresh, untouched, unseen,
Promises cherished, moments keen.

Laughter spills on the frozen ground,
Children dance, their joy unbound.
Every flake a wish to make,
In the silence, dreams awake.

As daylight fades, the dusk arrives,
Guide us gently, nature thrives.
In the first flurry, fate aligns,
And all is blanketed, where love shines.

Echos of a Frigid Twilight

At twilight's edge, the shadows creep,
Where whispers linger, secrets keep.
The cold embraces every breath,
In echoes soft, the day meets death.

Bare branches sway against the sky,
A hint of warmth as night draws nigh.
The chill primes the heart to soar,
In hushed tones, we crave for more.

Moonlight drapes the world in gray,
Stars awaken, shyly play.
Frigid winds and frozen dreams,
Sing of life through silver beams.

As darkness wraps the earth in grace,
Every corner finds its place.
In the stillness now resides,
The echoes of our heart's confides.

When the Wind Whispers Warnings

In autumn's breath, the wind does call,
With warnings wrapped, as leaves do fall.
Rustling secrets, tales from afar,
A symphony sung by each wandering star.

As dark clouds gather, shadows loom,
Nature speaks, foretelling doom.
Every gust a gentle plea,
Listen closely, and you will see.

Branches sway, a dance of fate,
The earth anticipates its state.
With every howl, a story told,
Of battles fought, of hearts so bold.

When the wind whispers, heed its song,
In nature's arms, we all belong.
Through storms we learn, through trials we rise,
In every warning, wisdom lies.

Glistening Hills of White

The hills are clad in purest snow,
Beneath the sun's soft, golden glow.
Each crystal sparkles, shines so bright,
A winter's dream, a breathtaking sight.

Footprints trace a winding way,
As laughter dances, children play.
In joy, we find our worries cease,
The glistening hills bring us sweet peace.

Nature's canvas, painted white,
A world transformed, a heart's delight.
The chill embraces, wraps us tight,
In snowy realms, we find our light.

With every turn, a new surprise,
The magic hidden 'neath the skies.
In every flake, a story told,
In glistening hills, our dreams unfold.

The Heartbeat of Frigid Days

In winter's grip, the world stands still,
The air is sharp, yet warm the thrill.
Each breath a cloud, each step a mark,
In frigid days, we find our spark.

The sun dips low, a golden ray,
A fleeting warmth, then fades away.
The icy winds, they call our name,
In chilly breath, we feel the same.

Trees stand tall, their branches bare,
Yet in the silence, beauty's there.
The frozen lake, a mirror's play,
Reflecting time on frigid days.

Together we embrace the cold,
In stories shared, our hearts are bold.
With every heartbeat, life persists,
In winter's chill, we're wrapped in bliss.

Frostbite Whispers

In shadows deep, the whispers call,
Of frost and chill that cloak us all.
The night's embrace, both soft and keen,
A tale of winter, crisp and clean.

Each flake that falls, a gentle kiss,
A fleeting moment, wrapped in bliss.
The wind's sharp song, a haunting tune,
Beneath the watchful, silver moon.

Footfalls echo on frozen streets,
As every heartbeat softly greets.
In whispers light, the stories weave,
Of frostbite's art, we dare believe.

Concealed in darkness, secrets hum,
In winter's heart, the stillness comes.
Through frosted breath, we whisper low,
The magic found in all this snow.

Chills and Thrills of the Frozen Night

The frozen night, a canvas vast,
With frosty breath, the moments cast.
Each star above, a diamond bright,
In chilly air, we feel delight.

A crackling fire, warmth draws near,
As stories bloom, we share our cheer.
The world outside, a silent play,
As night unveils its shivering sway.

With every gust, the thrill ignites,
Adventures beckon in moonlit sights.
The cold's embrace, a daring call,
To chase the dreams that inside thrall.

In laughter shared, the heart ignites,
Through chills and thrills of winter nights.
Together bound by warmth and light,
We dance and sing in pure delight.

Crisp Air and Warm Hearts

Crisp air whispers softly,
Through the trees where shadows lie.
Warm hearts gather close,
As golden leaves drift by.

Laughter fills the twilight,
Echoing through the chill.
Fires crackle with delight,
Time slows, the world is still.

Blankets wrap us tightly,
Stories weave through the night.
Crisp air brings us closer,
To share in the soft light.

With each gentle heartbeat,
We embrace this fleeting hour.
Crisp air and warm hearts,
Nature's sweetest power.

Snowbound Secrets

Snowflakes gently flutter,
Covering the world in white.
Secrets hide in silence,
Underneath the starry night.

Footsteps print the fresh snow,
Leading to paths unknown.
Whispers of the winter,
In a language all our own.

Crisp echoes of the past,
Mingle with a frosty breeze.
Snowbound dreams awaken,
Wrapped in soft memories.

As twilight dims the sky,
We find warmth in the cold.
Snowbound secrets linger,
In stories yet untold.

The Icebound Diary of Dreams

In the icebound diary,
Of dreams both lost and found,
Each page tells a story,
Wrapped in a winter's sound.

Frosted words take shape,
Dancing like the northern lights.
Whispers of forgotten hope,
On cold, starry nights.

Every glance of moonlight,
Unfolds a frozen scene.
Magic woven within,
In the places we have been.

The ink is made of snow,
And the pen, a silver star.
In the icebound diary,
We wander near and far.

A Constellation of Frosted Nights

Underneath the starlight,
Frost bites the silent air.
A constellation glimmers,
Of dreams we love to share.

Every twinkle tells a tale,
Of moments lost in time.
Frosted nights embrace us,
In a rhythm, pure and prime.

The world feels so enchanted,
Wrapped in winter's glow.
As we weave our wishes,
Beneath the stars aglow.

A constellation of frost,
Whispers secrets of the night.
In our hearts, it lingers,
A beautiful, shining light.

A Dance of Ice and Light

In twilight's embrace, shadows cast,
Whispers of winter, bright and vast.
Crystals twirl in a shimmering show,
Nature's ballet, a soft, gentle glow.

Glistening frost on the boughs of trees,
Waltzing with winds, a delicate breeze.
Moonbeams shimmer, reflecting the night,
In the silence, a dance of pure light.

Snowflakes flutter, each one unique,
Gentle reminders of what we seek.
As the night holds, our hearts take flight,
In this wonder, all feels just right.

A canvas painted in shades of white,
The world transformed, a breathtaking sight.
Under the stars, with joy, we unite,
In this dance of ice and light.

The Stillness Beneath the Snow

A blanket of white, so soft and deep,
Hides the earth from its restless sleep.
Whispers of dreams in the frosty air,
Encased in silence, a world laid bare.

The trees stand tall with arms open wide,
Guardians of secrets the snow can't hide.
Each branch wears diamonds, a sparkling crown,
In this tranquil hush, we gather 'round.

Time seems to pause, as moments blend,
Nature's soft lullaby, a soothing friend.
In the stillness, we breathe in the peace,
Yearning hearts find solace; worries cease.

Though winter's chill bites, we hold it dear,
For beneath the frost lies the warmth of cheer.
In snowy repose, we find our way,
Through the stillness beneath the snow, we stay.

Frosty Footprints on the Path

With every step on the sparkling trail,
Frosty footprints weave a winter tale.
Each crunch beneath brings memories alive,
In the morning light, our spirits thrive.

The world transformed, as if in a dream,
Nature paints landscapes with glistening gleam.
Whispers of magic in the icy air,
Trace our journey with love and care.

A dance of shadows where the sunbeam lies,
Paths intersect, beneath the broad skies.
Every footprint tells of the joys we sought,
In the quiet of winter, our hearts are caught.

As seasons shift, the memory stays,
Footsteps in frost guide us always.
Through meadows and woods where the silence calls,
We leave our mark as the soft snow falls.

Echoes of Shimmering Chill

In twilight's glow, the world shines bright,
Echoes of chill, a stunning sight.
Each breath we take is a cloud of white,
In the heart of winter, we find delight.

The frozen lake, a mirror of dreams,
Under the stars, it silently gleams.
Whispers of frost dance in the air,
A symphony played without a care.

As nights grow long and days go slow,
Stories unfold in the gentle snow.
Wrapped in warmth, we gather near,
In echoes of chill, we share our cheer.

From mountain tops to valley deep,
The world awakes from its winter sleep.
In each chilly breath, we find our thrill,
As we listen close to the echoes of chill.

The Breath of a Frozen Whisper

In the stillness of the night,
A breath escapes, so soft and light.
Frozen whispers in the air,
Secrets kept beyond compare.

Moonlit shadows dance and glide,
Where dreams and echoes gently collide.
Silent voices, crisp and clear,
Haunting melodies we long to hear.

Frosted branches sway with grace,
Nature's song in a frozen space.
Each note a soft, enchanting thrill,
Captured by the night's own chill.

A lullaby of winter's breath,
The stillness sings of life and death.
With every sigh, the night will share,
The whispers lost in frozen air.

Snow-covered Secrets

Beneath the blanket, soft and white,
Lies the world in tranquil light.
Hidden stories, lost from view,
A tapestry of shades and hue.

Footprints linger, then are gone,
Weaving tales until the dawn.
Whispers hush as shadows roam,
In the snow, we find our home.

Every flake a wish, a dream,
Turning life into a gleam.
Snow-covered secrets safe and sound,
Waiting for the spring to be found.

Softly falling, kisses sweet,
Nature's magic at our feet.
In the silence, truths emerge,
From snow-covered lands, they surge.

Dreaming Beneath the Ice

Beneath the surface, still and cold,
Lies a world of stories untold.
Dreams are sleeping, held in thrall,
Waiting for the thaw to call.

Rippling currents, hidden deep,
Silent promises they keep.
In the shadows, hope remains,
Beneath the ice, life still reigns.

Tickling bubbles dance and rise,
Whispers of wonders in disguise.
Each breath beneath, a sacred vow,
A promise made to the here and now.

When the sun breaks through the ice,
Awakening spirits, oh so nice.
Dreaming ceases, time stands still,
Beneath the ice, the heart will thrill.

Blanket of Frost

A blanket of frost covers the ground,
In crystal layers, silence surrounds.
Nature's breath, a gentle sigh,
Embracing beauty as days go by.

Stars glisten bright in the chilled sky,
Whispering secrets, oh so high.
Frozen gardens, blooms of white,
Glistening softly in the night.

Every spark, a fleeting chance,
Needing warmth in the moonlit dance.
Frosty fingers gently weave,
A tapestry of dreams to believe.

Underneath this shimmering veil,
A world awaits with tales to tell.
Wrapped in wonder, soft and vast,
A precious moment, destined to pass.

Frosted Lullabies at Dusk

Whispers of winter softly call,
As shadows stretch and darkness falls.
The stars awaken, twinkling bright,
In the embrace of a serene night.

Gentle flakes begin to dance,
Each flurry a fleeting, delicate chance.
Crystals cradle the world in white,
Singing lullabies to the night.

Dreams weave through the glimmering air,
In the chilly hush, worries bare.
Frosted whispers tuck in the trees,
As snowflakes drift on the winter breeze.

Sleep now, dear heart, let go of your fears,
For lullabies echo through the years.
In the frosted calm, find your rest,
Under the cloak of winter's best.

Hibernation's Melancholy

Beneath layers of snow, silence reigns,
The world lies still, wrapped in chains.
Nature's heartbeat slows to a sigh,
As dreams of spring in slumber lie.

Shadows stretch across the ground,
In solitude, lost ways are found.
Animals curl in their cozy dens,
While the moon watches, the night begins.

Cold winds whisper tales of the past,
Of seasons gone, too bright, too fast.
Time lingers in this somber space,
Longing for warmth's sweet embrace.

Yet in this stillness, hope resides,
Awaiting the thaw as time abides.
For all that sleeps shall one day rise,
Beneath the sun's welcoming skies.

The Bite of the Frost King

From icy heights, the Frost King reigns,
With a breath that cools, and stings like chains.
His finger trails create the frost,
On homes and hearts, all warmth is lost.

The landscape shimmers, sharp and bold,
Wrapped in whispers of bitter cold.
He dances on rooftops, a wintry sprite,
Turning joy into a frozen fright.

Yet beneath his chill, life quietly sighs,
Waiting for spring against darkened skies.
The bite may sting, but it does not break,
For every frost, a promise wakes.

With each sunrise, the grip will fade,
As nature's beauty is unmade.
The Frost King bows to the warming sun,
And with his retreat, life has begun.

Numbed Embrace of the Arctic

In the hushed expanse of the endless white,
Where day melts softly into night.
The Arctic breathes in a frozen trance,
Wrapped in quiet, a tranquil dance.

Icebergs drift like thoughts on the breeze,
Silent whispers among ancient trees.
The air is crisp, a biting thrill,
A realm where time stands still.

A muted canvas, vast and grand,
Each snowflake's artwork, nature's hand.
Under the moonlight's silvery glow,
A dreamscape where only the brave dare go.

Yet in this numbness, beauty thrives,
Reminding all that stillness survives.
Embrace the chill, let peace unfold,
In the Arctic's heart, where stories are told.

Frosty Footprints on Forgotten Paths

In the hush of winter's breath,
Footsteps vanish, a fleeting death.
Each impression, a tale untold,
Whispers of journeys, brave and bold.

Beneath the trees, shadows play,
Frosted memories fade away.
A silent witness to nature's art,
Frosty footprints leave a mark.

The echoing crunch, a ghostly sound,
Lost in the woods where hope is found.
Paths entwined with dreams of old,
Adventures longingly retold.

With every step, the chill embraces,
Revealing earth's forgotten places.
A dance of seasons, time moves on,
Yet traces linger, though they're gone.

A Symphony of Snowflakes

Softly drifting through the air,
Snowflakes twirl without a care.
Each one sparkles, unique in grace,
A silent song, a quiet space.

Harmonies hum as they descend,
Nature's gift, a wondrous blend.
Kissing rooftops, fields, and trees,
Creating laughter, whispers, and peace.

Children rush to greet the flurry,
Building dreams in perfect hurry.
A flake lands gently on a nose,
In joy and wonder, the heart knows.

When night falls, the world is still,
Blanketed under a winter chill.
A symphony of silence plays,
In snowy realms, where magic stays.

Beneath the Weight of White

Under layers of frozen dreams,
The world sleeps softly, or so it seems.
Blankets piled high upon the ground,
In pristine silence, beauty is found.

Trees bend low with a heavy crown,
Cradling memories, a reflective gown.
Footsteps muffled, whispers hushed,
Nature pauses, in peace, we're brushed.

Icicles hang like crystal tears,
Catching sunlight through the years.
Each drip a promise of warmer days,
While winter wraps us in a cool embrace.

With every breath, the air is crisp,
Holding magic within its wisp.
Beneath the weight of white so pure,
Lies a world where dreams endure.

Icicles Hanging like Time's Tickers

Like clock hands frozen in their flight,
Icicles hang in the fading light.
Time suspended, a moment caught,
Nature's art, with silence wrought.

Dripping slowly, a measured grace,
Each drop a heartbeat, in this space.
They shimmer softly, a glinting show,
Marking the passage of time below.

Beneath a canopy of snow-white dreams,
Frozen memories hang in streams.
Nature's timer, a patient guide,
In icy stillness, the world will bide.

With every thaw, the truth will flow,
Icicles melt, letting go.
Yet in their beauty, we find our way,
Through winter's night, to the warmth of day.

Shivers Beneath a Silver Veil

A frost creeps softly through the night,
The moon hangs low, a beacon bright.
Whispers of wind dance in the trees,
Chill on my skin, a haunting breeze.

Veils of silver, pure and deep,
While shadows linger, secrets keep.
Each breath a cloud, each step a chance,
Lost in the dream of a wintry dance.

Footprints fade on glistening ground,
In solitude, silence resounds.
Sculpted snowflakes, intricate art,
Melting slowly, they break my heart.

Beneath a sky, so vast, so wide,
I feel the night as my only guide.
In shivers, I find a cloak of peace,
While the world in stillness, holds its fleece.

Cold Snap Serenade

A sudden chill, the air turns sharp,
Nature's breath, a frozen harp.
Notes of winter fill the air,
Echoing softly, everywhere.

Brittle branches, creaking low,
Crystals shimmer, a fleeting glow.
Underneath this frigid shroud,
I sing my song, though soft, not loud.

Gather round, the frost will play,
In melodic tones, night turns to day.
Each flake a note, each gust a sound,
In this cold snap, warmth is found.

Dance with me in the moonlit hue,
As winter whispers, sweet and true.
Together in this frozen trance,
In harmony, we start to dance.

Glistening Dreams of Ice

In the morning light, a world transformed,
Where every breath is crisp and warmed.
Shadows stretch in the glowing dawn,
While frozen dreams continue on.

Mirror lakes reflect the sky,
With silent edges, where echoes lie.
I walk on glass beneath my feet,
The icy whispers, soft and sweet.

Glistening branches, a fairy tale,
Tales of wonder in the pale.
Each sparkle sings the songs of yore,
In frozen vistas, we explore.

Through frosted fields, I wander wide,
Chasing light, where secrets hide.
In dreams of ice, my heart takes flight,
Wrapped in the beauty of winter's night.

When the World Went Gray

The sun bid farewell, the skies turned dim,
Clouds rolled in, a muted hymn.
Color drained from the vibrant day,
As shadows whispered, the world went gray.

Raindrops fell like tears from height,
Each droplet adding to the night.
Pavements glisten, wet and worn,
In this grayness, I feel reborn.

Hues of silver, charcoal, and mist,
A palette kissed by an artist's twist.
Beneath the gloom, I find my way,
In every moment, life's ballet.

And in this stillness, I hear a call,
In whispers of gray, I stand tall.
When the world went gray, it taught me to see,
Beauty lies where shadows can be.

Milton Keynes UK
Ingram Content Group UK Ltd.
UKHW022010131124
451149UK00013B/1093

9 789916 942895